welcome to coloring book alphabet

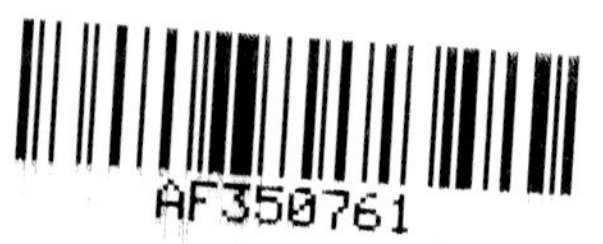

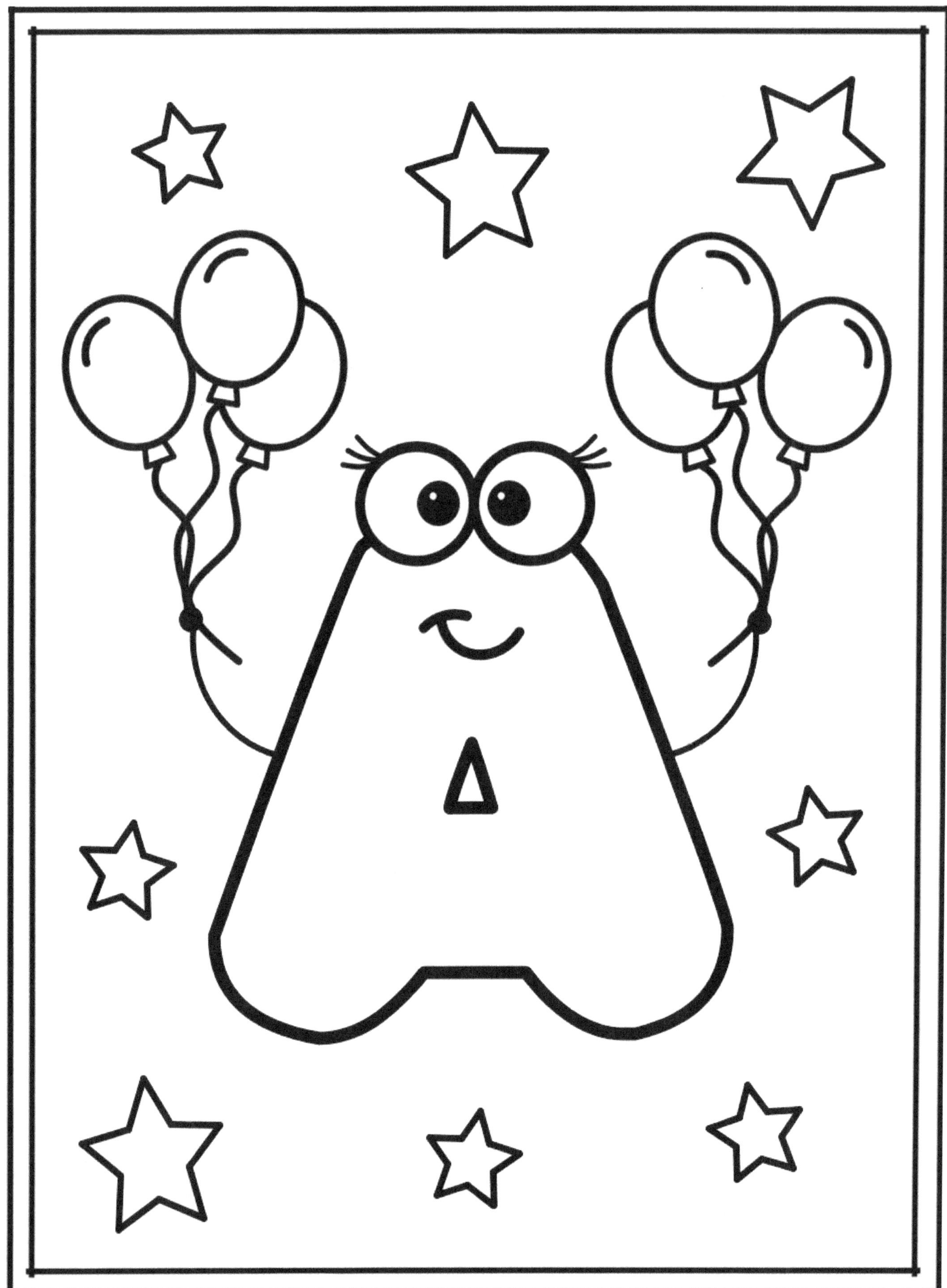

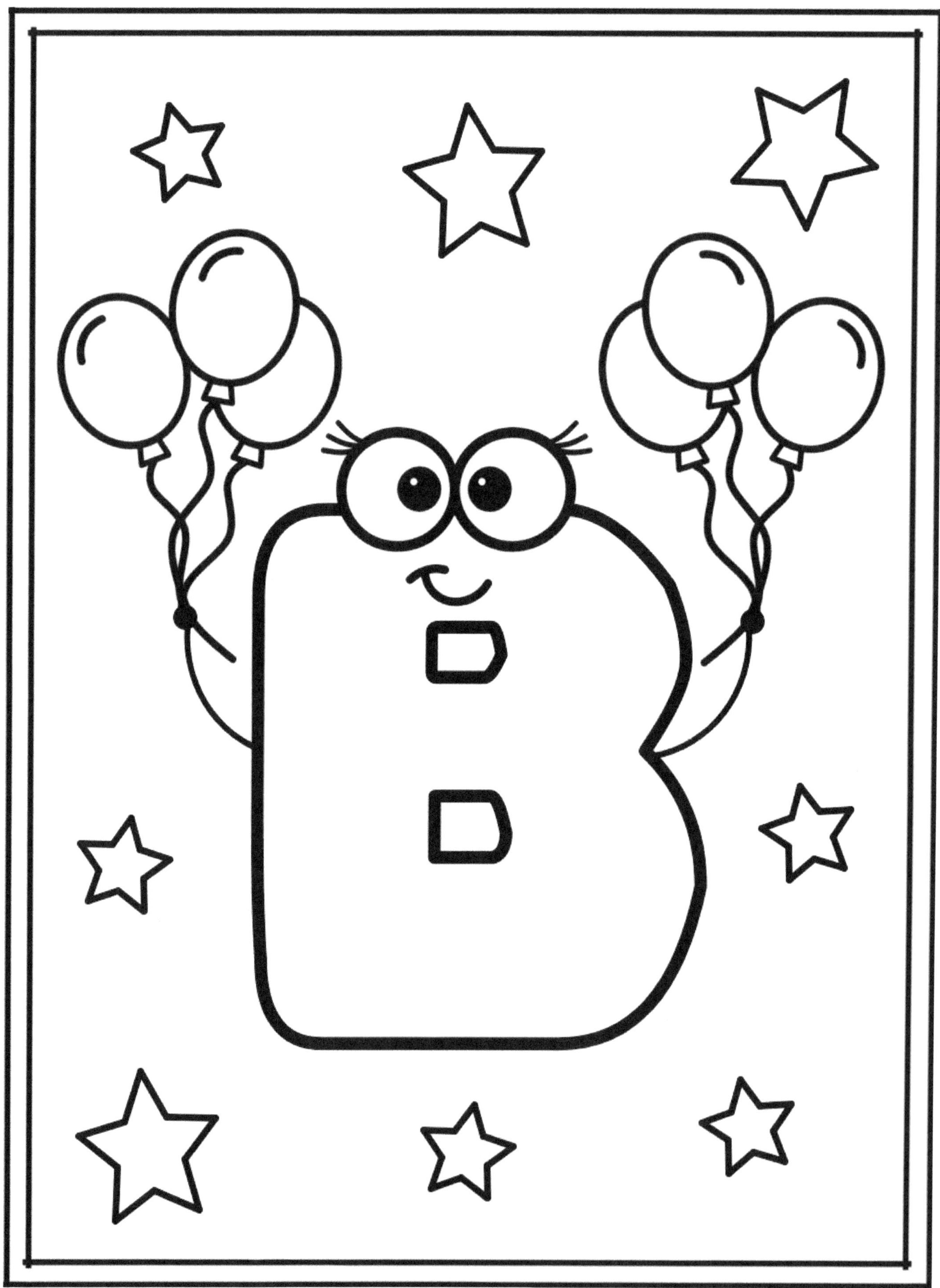

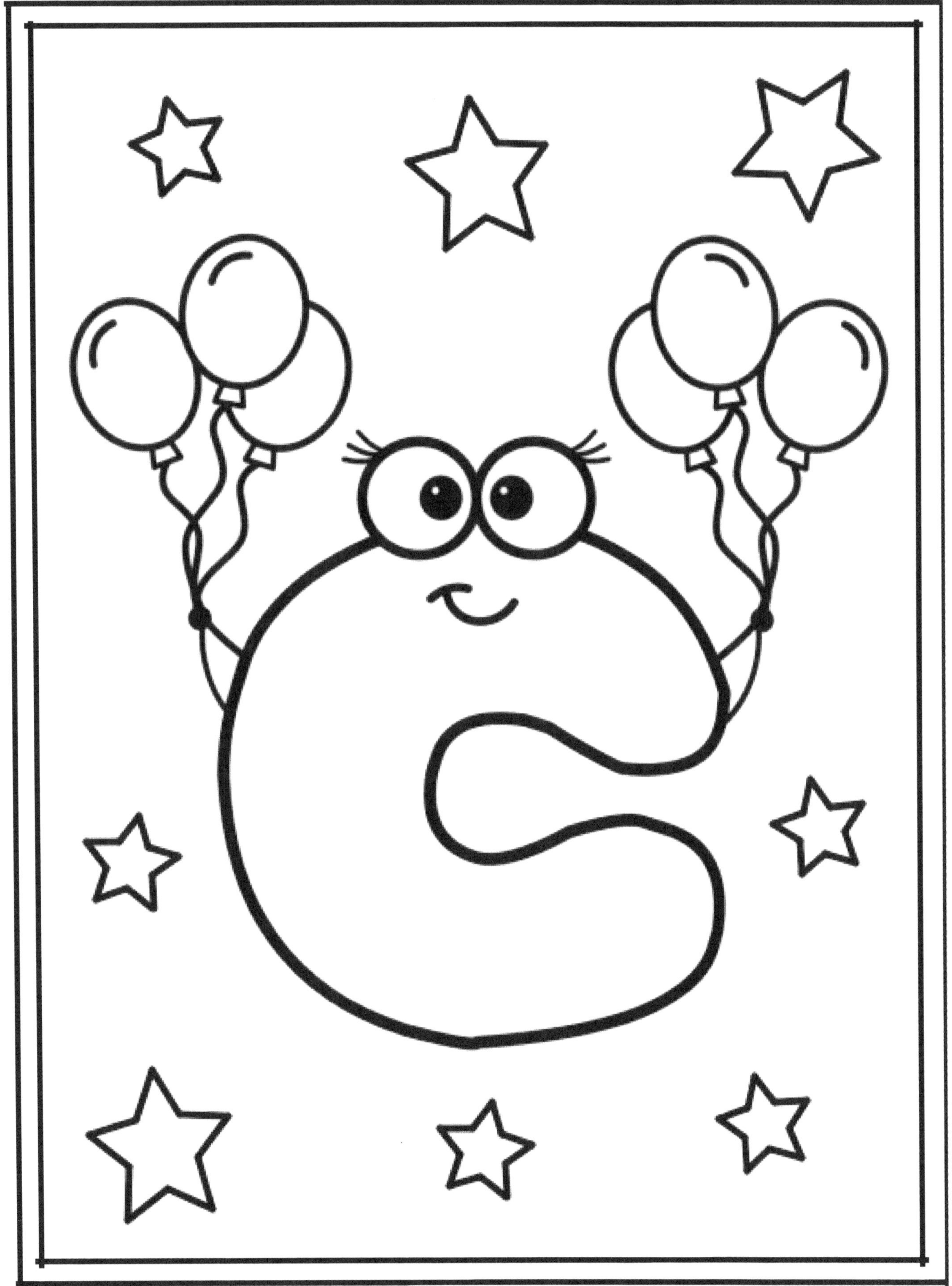

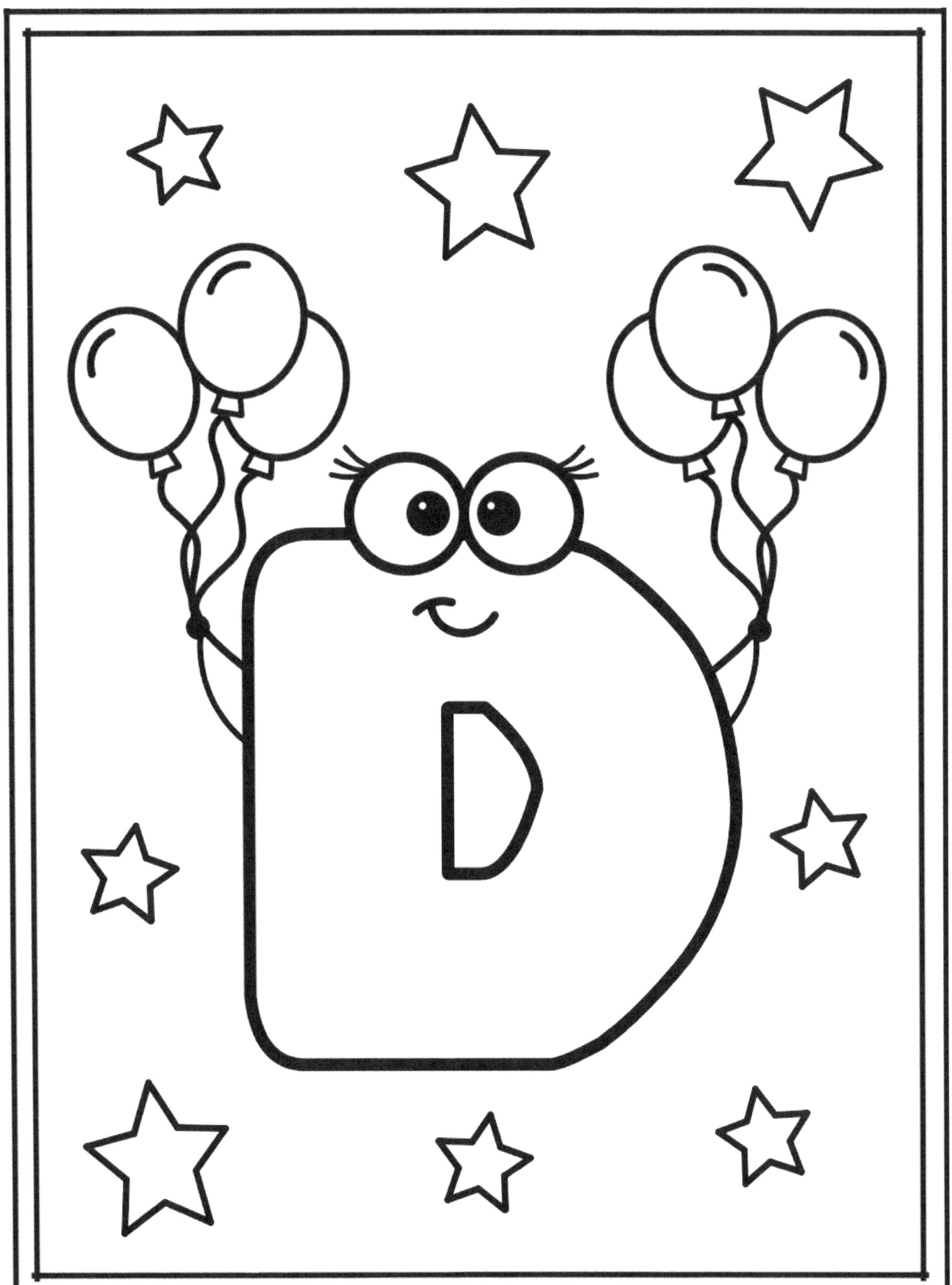

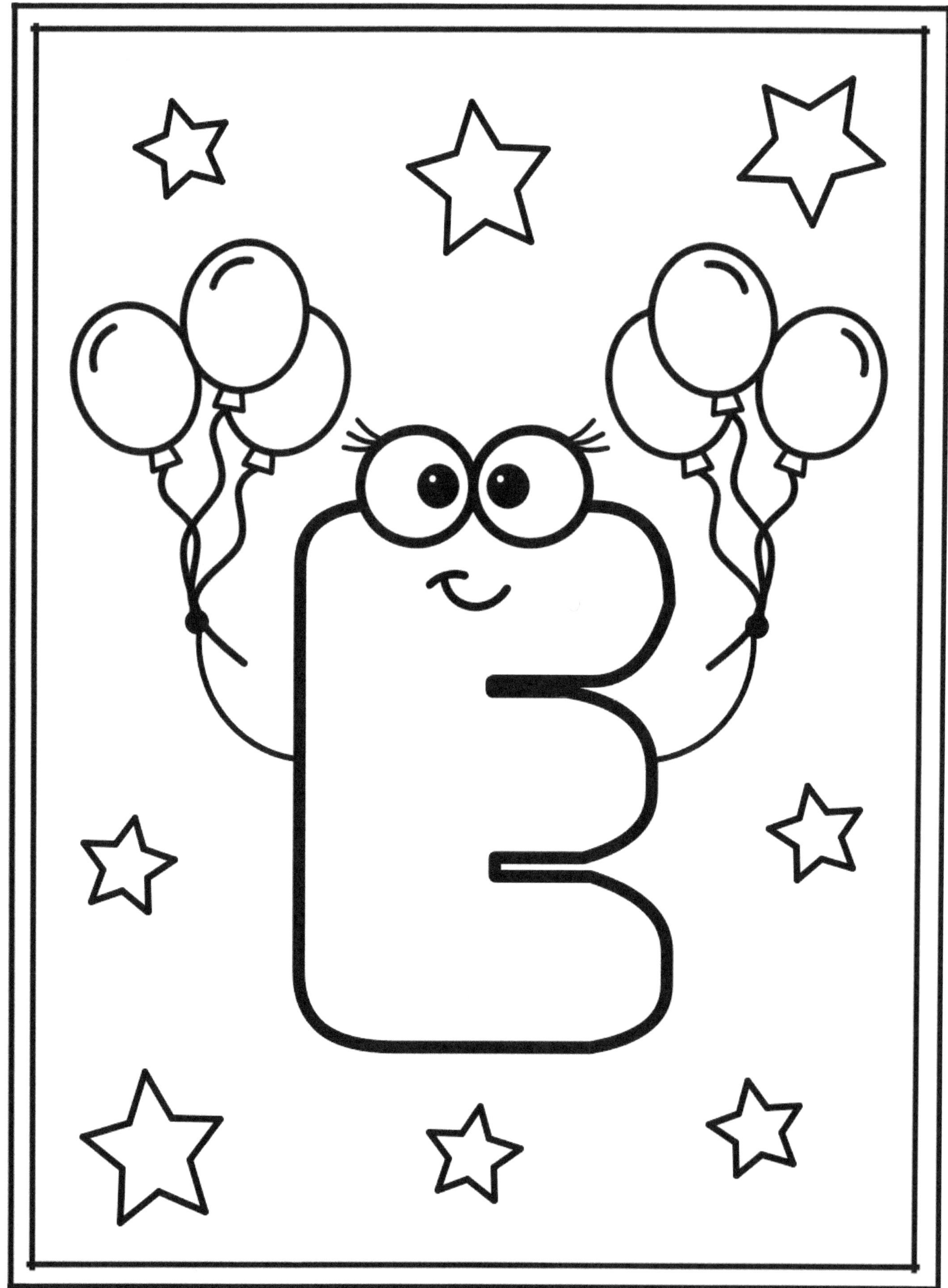

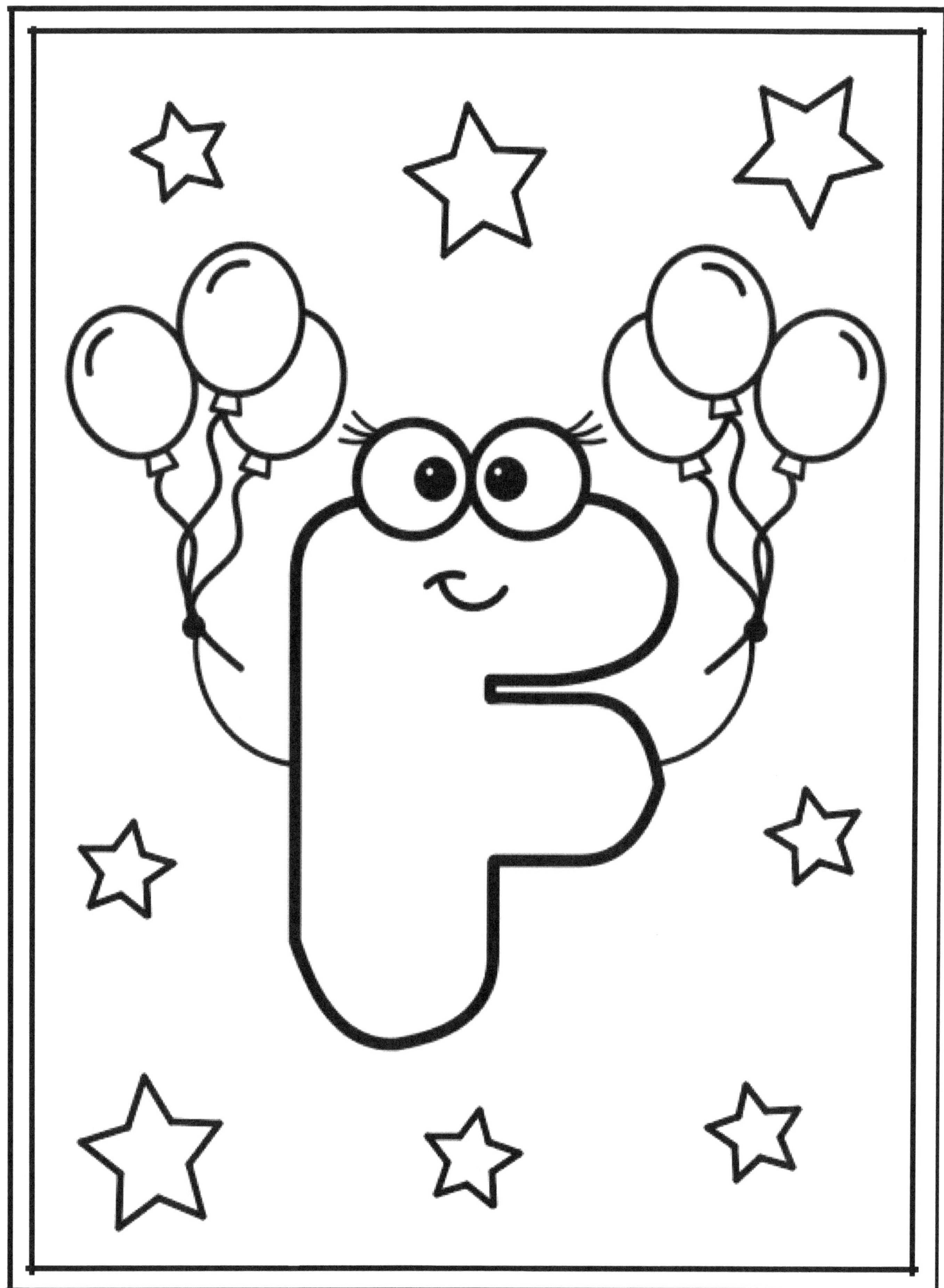

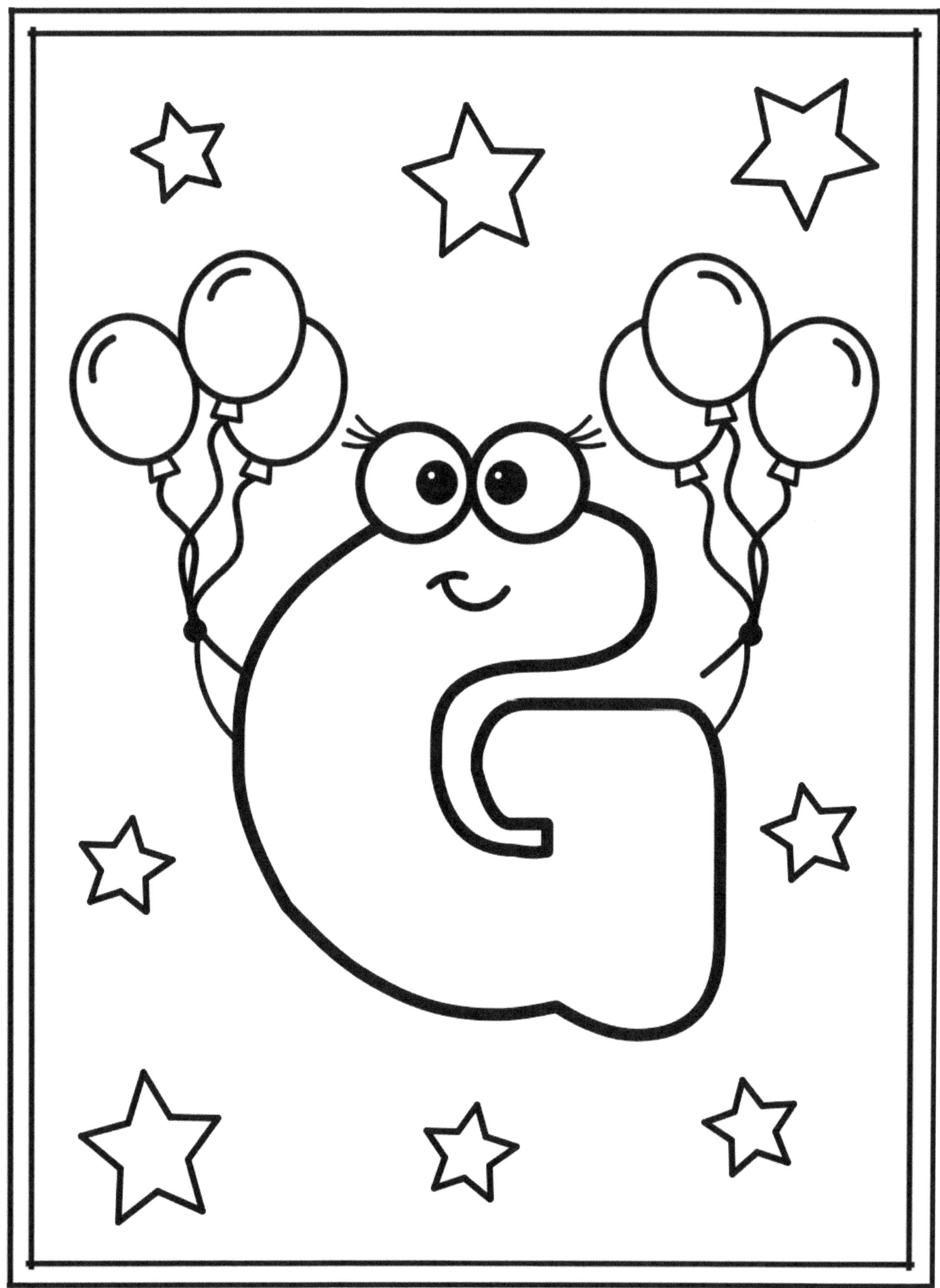

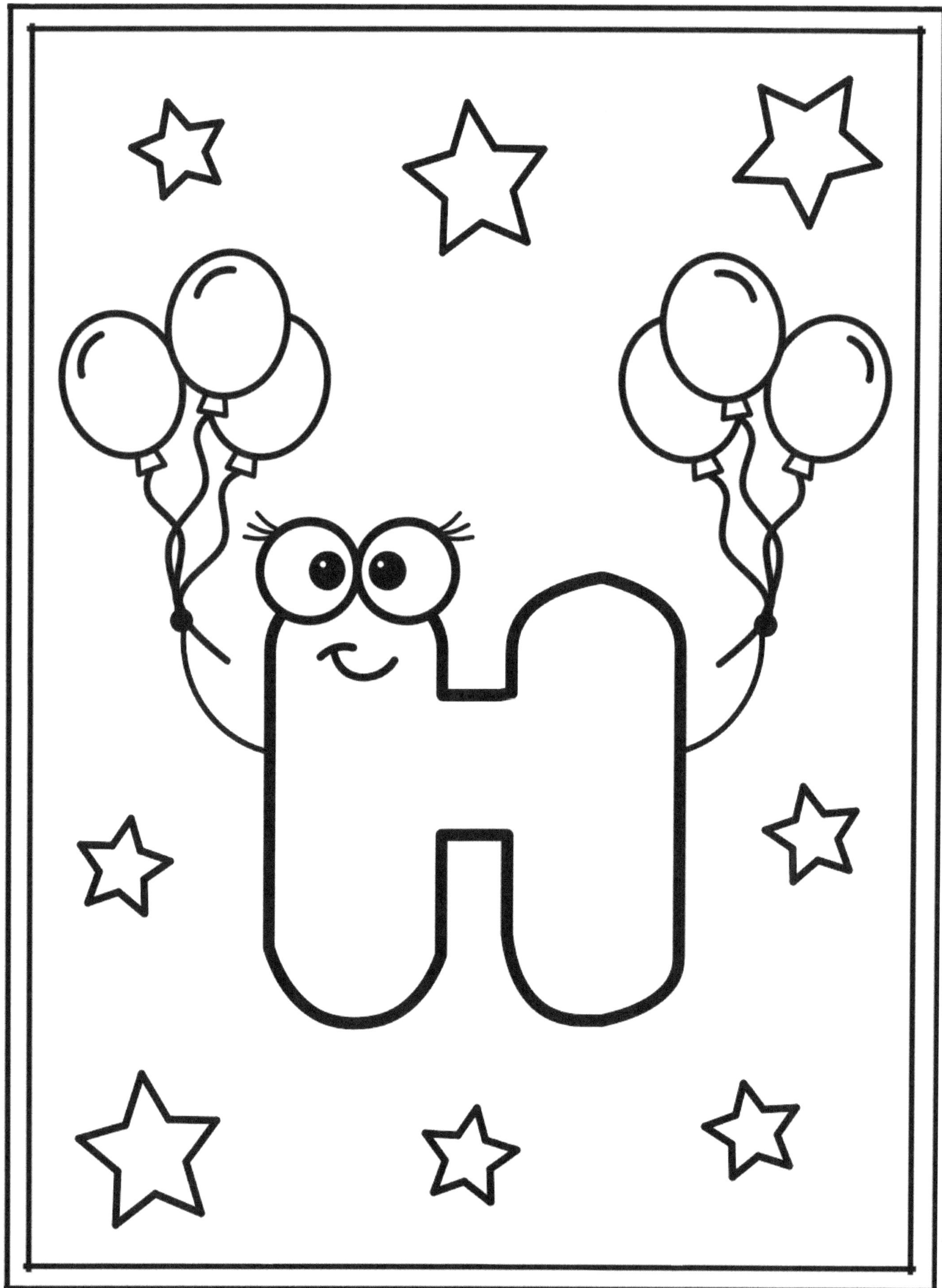

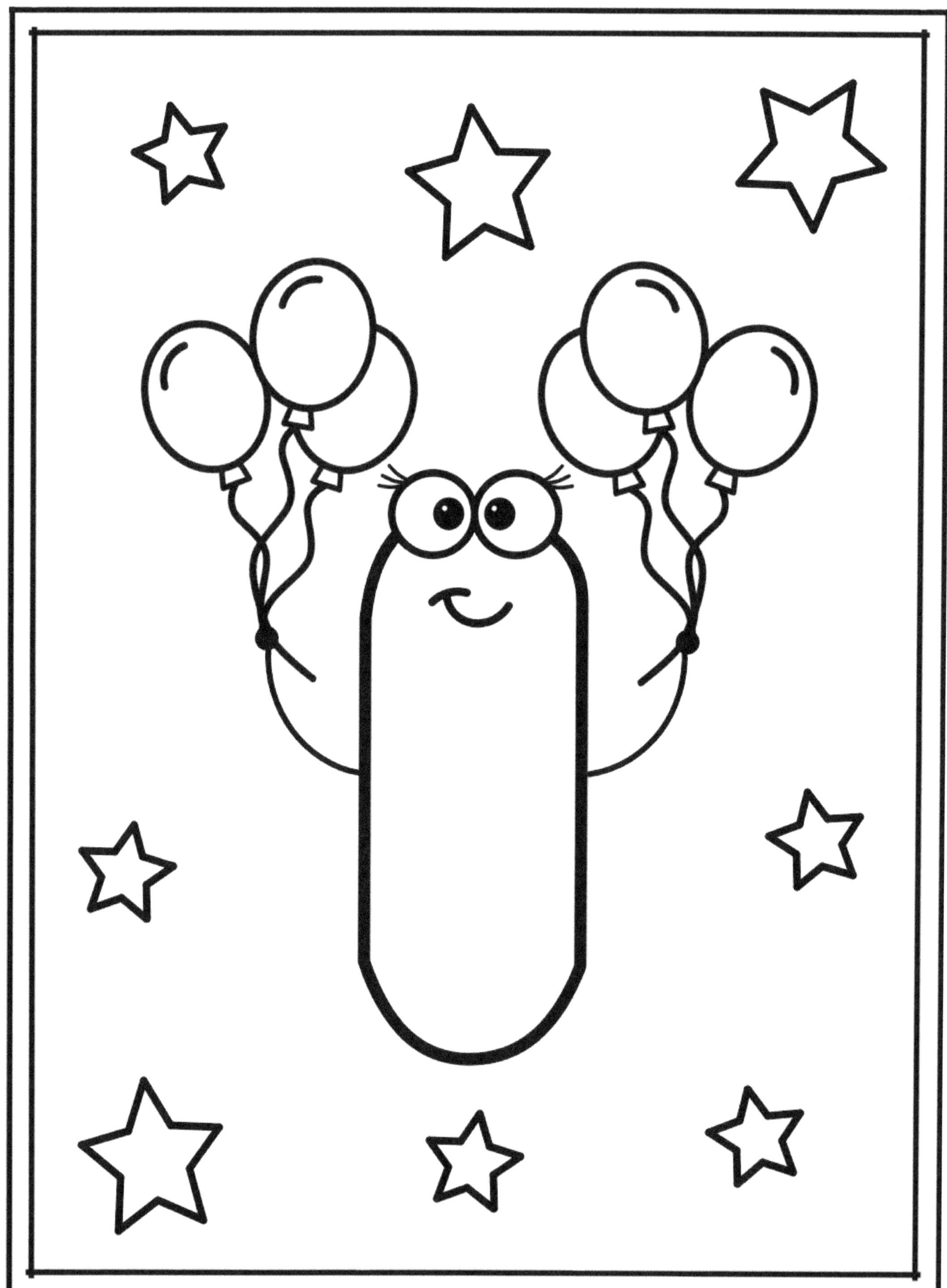

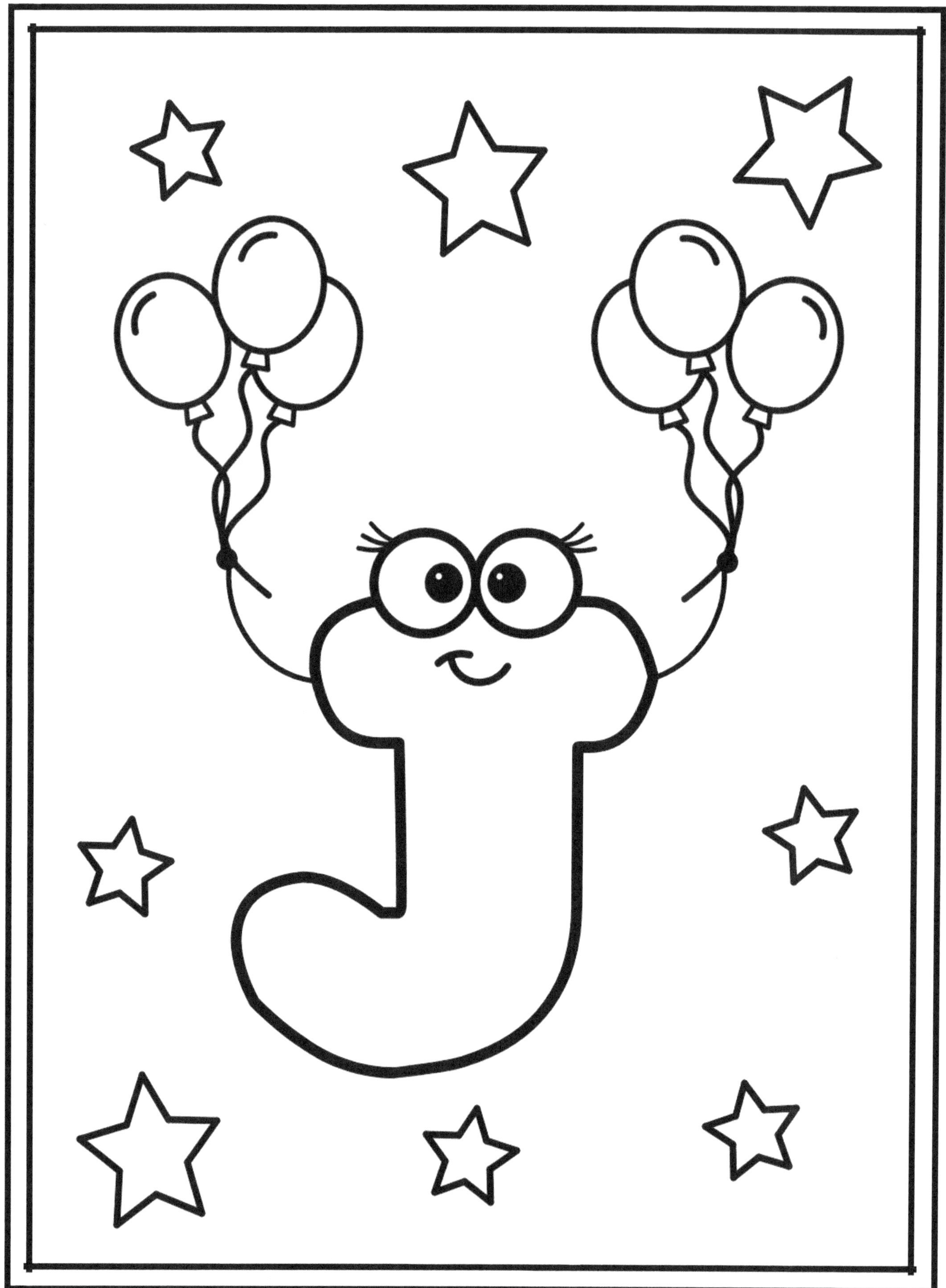

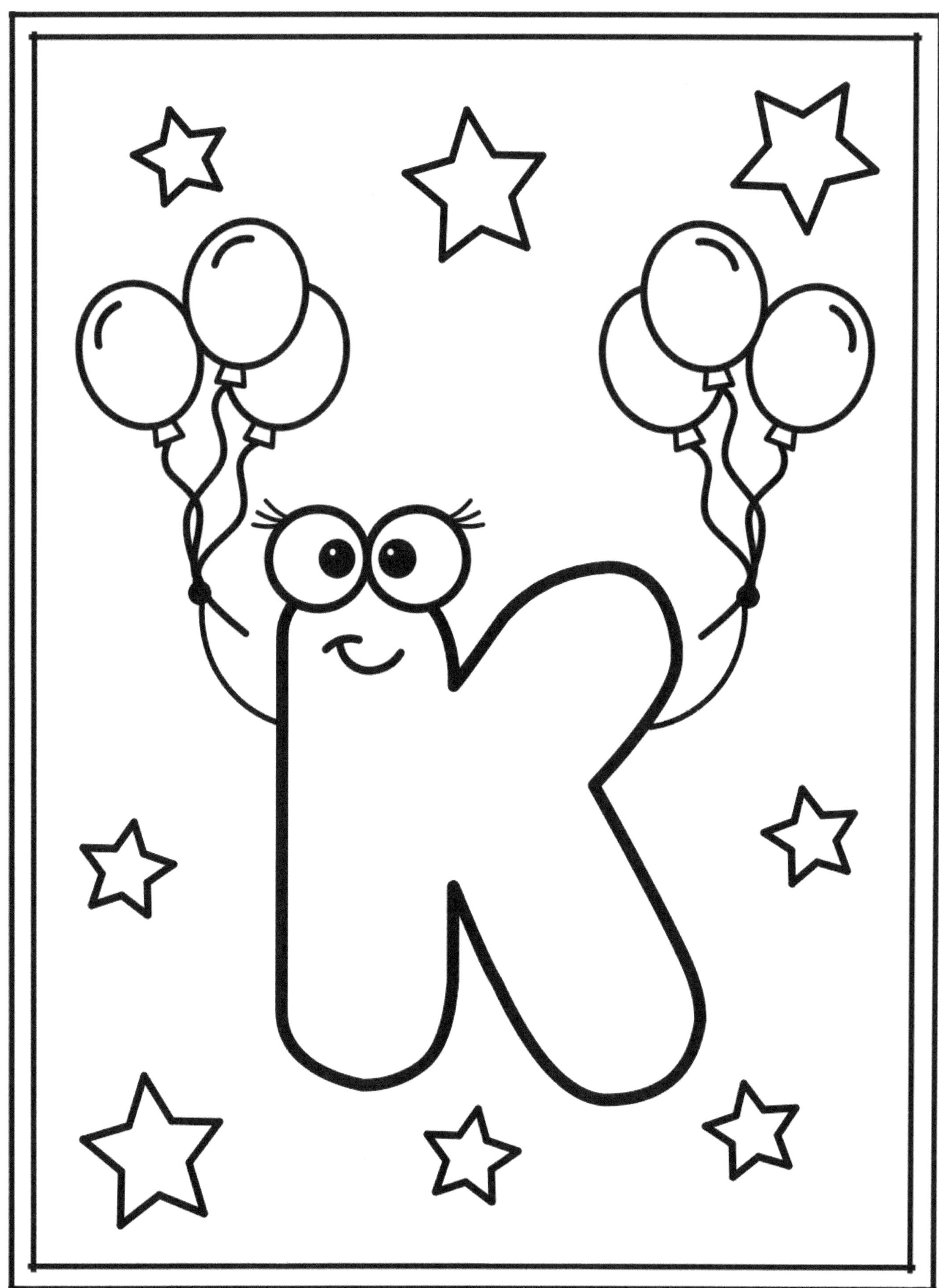
K

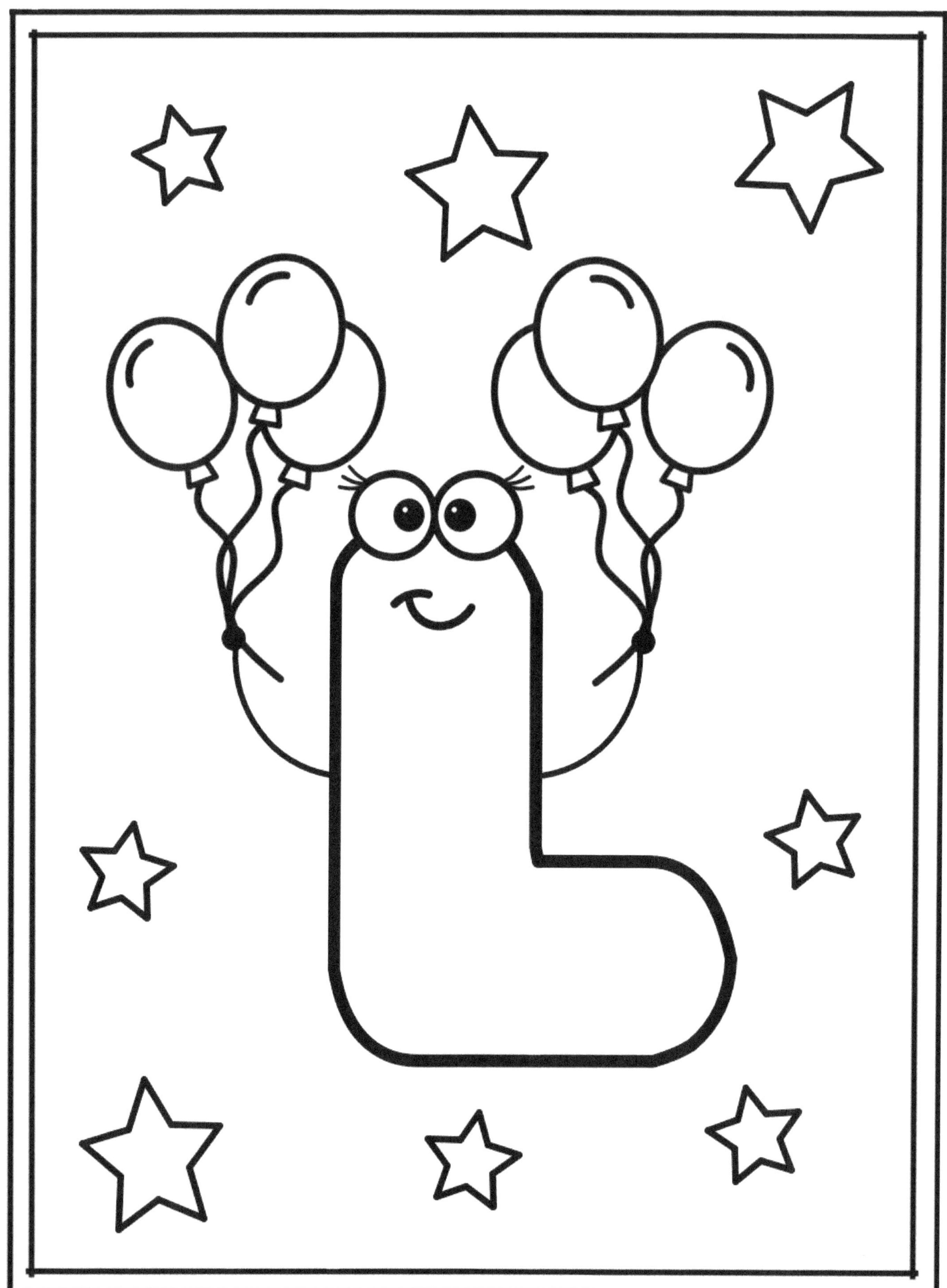

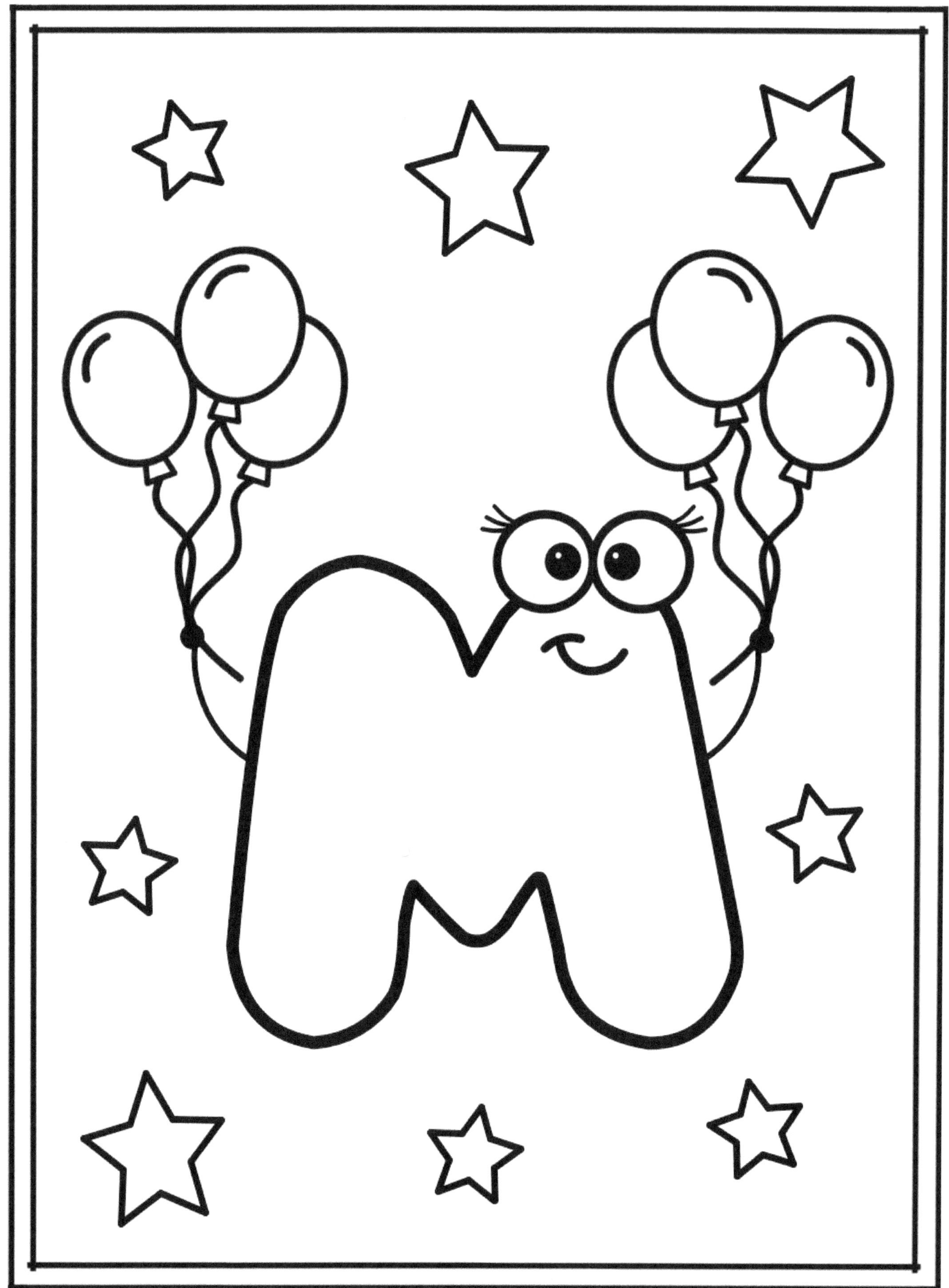

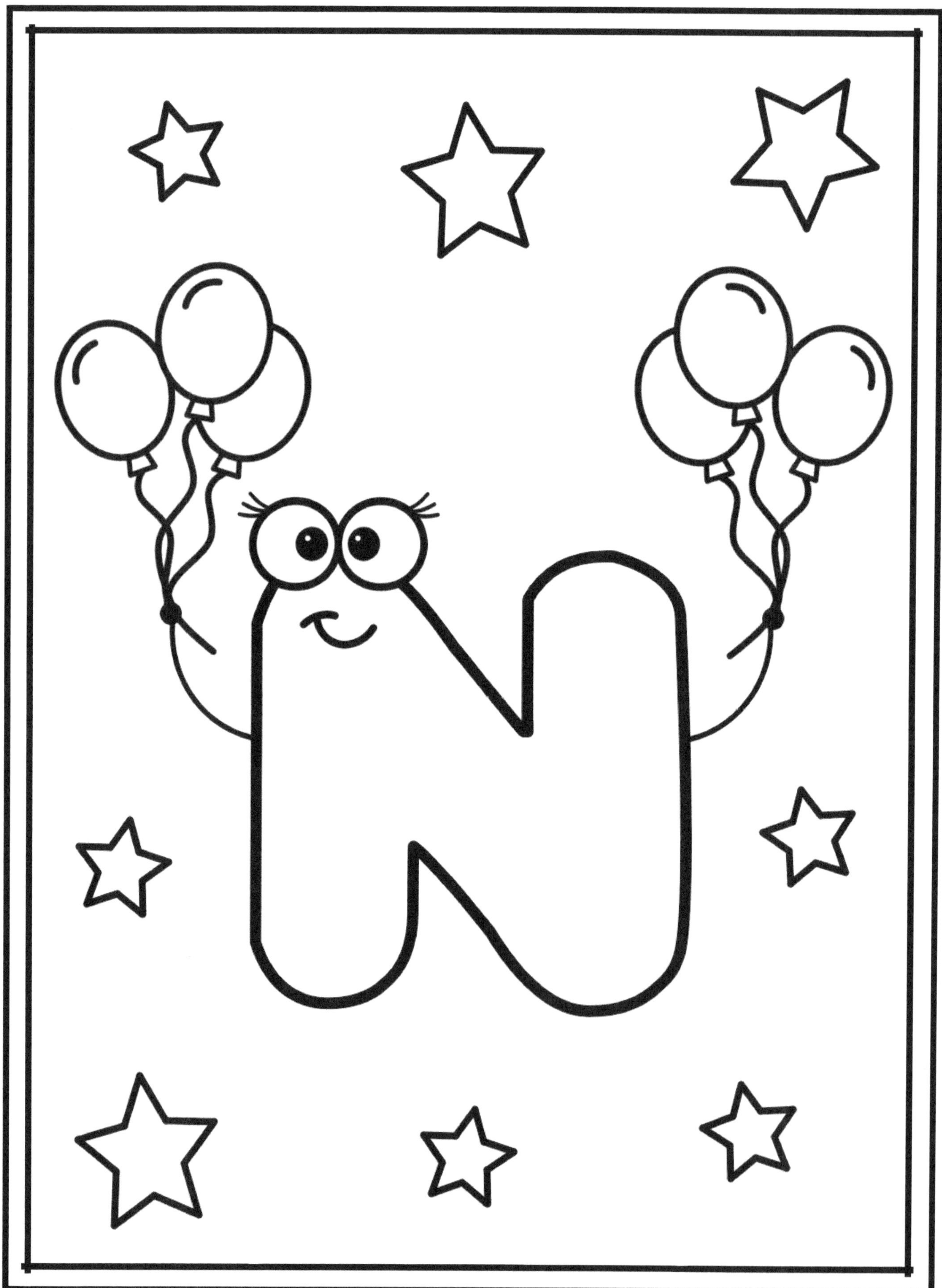

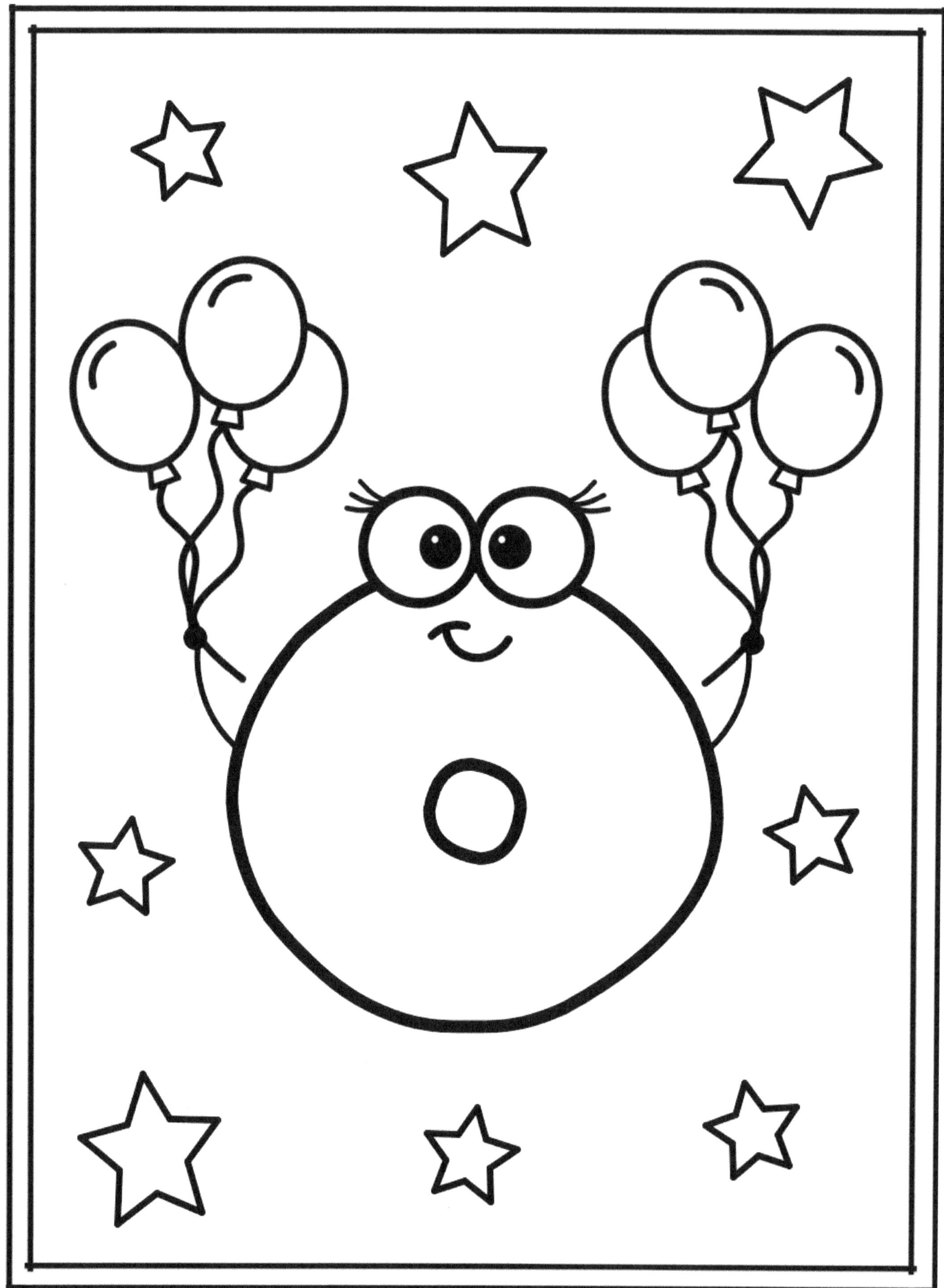

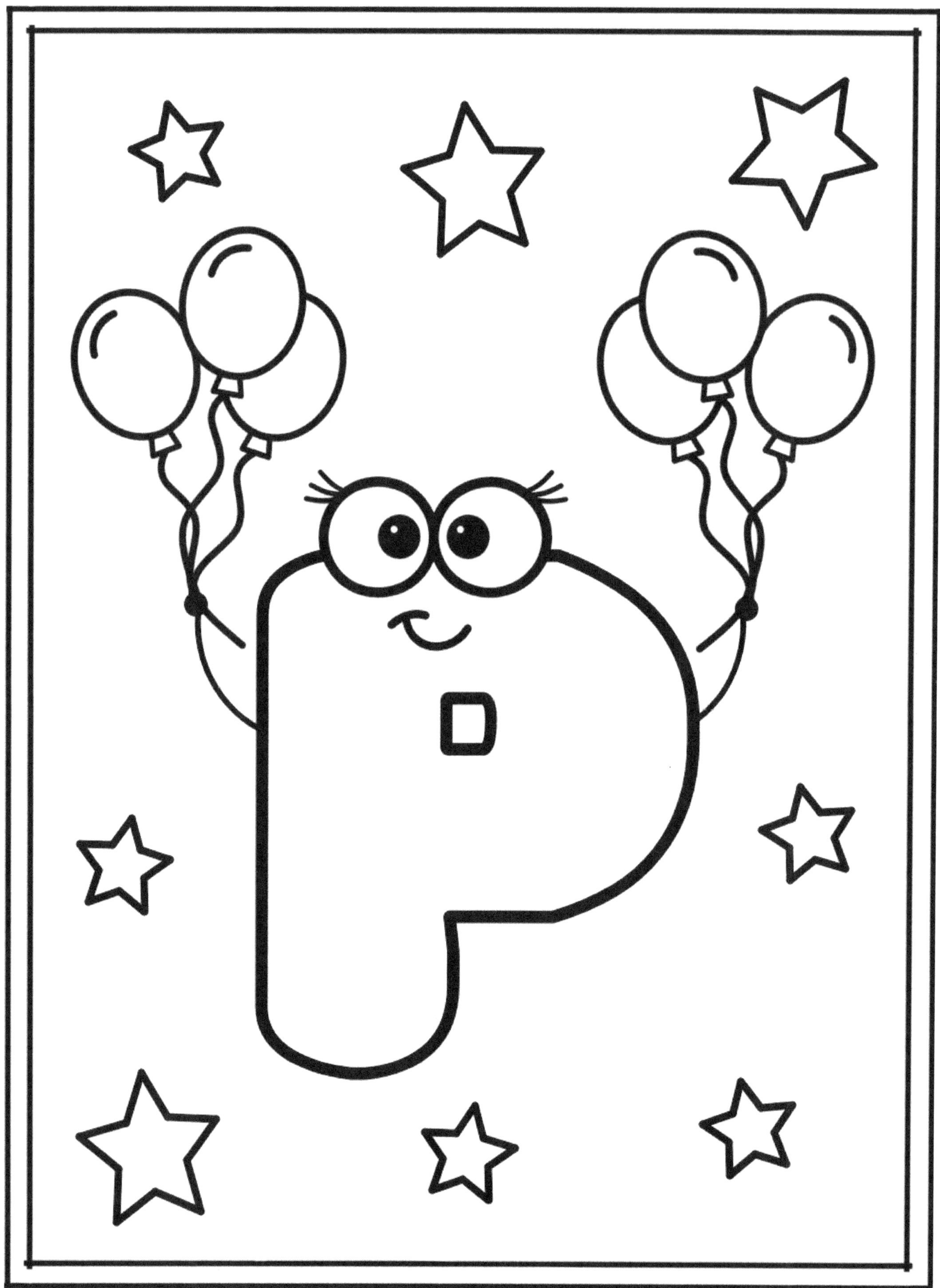

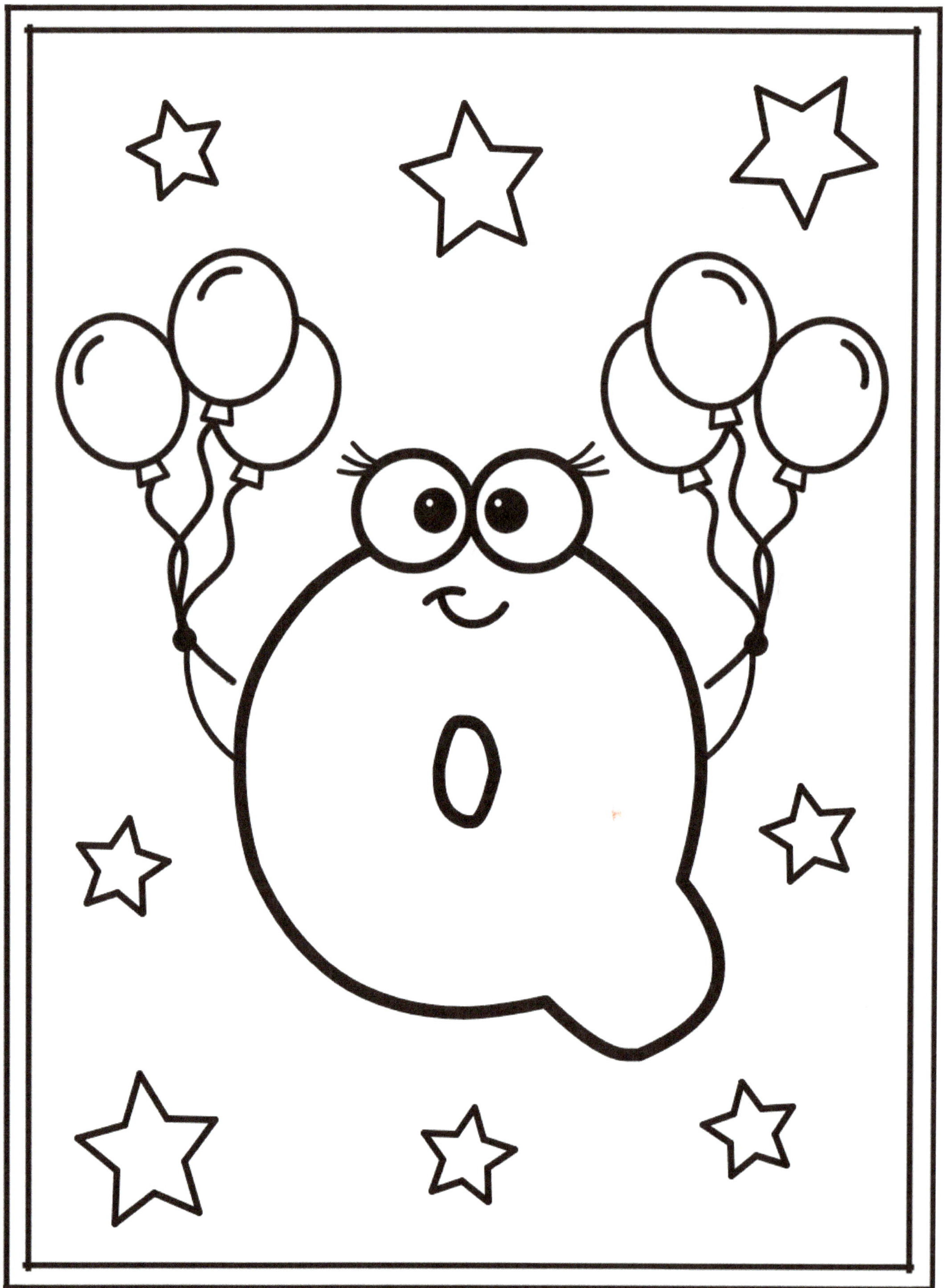

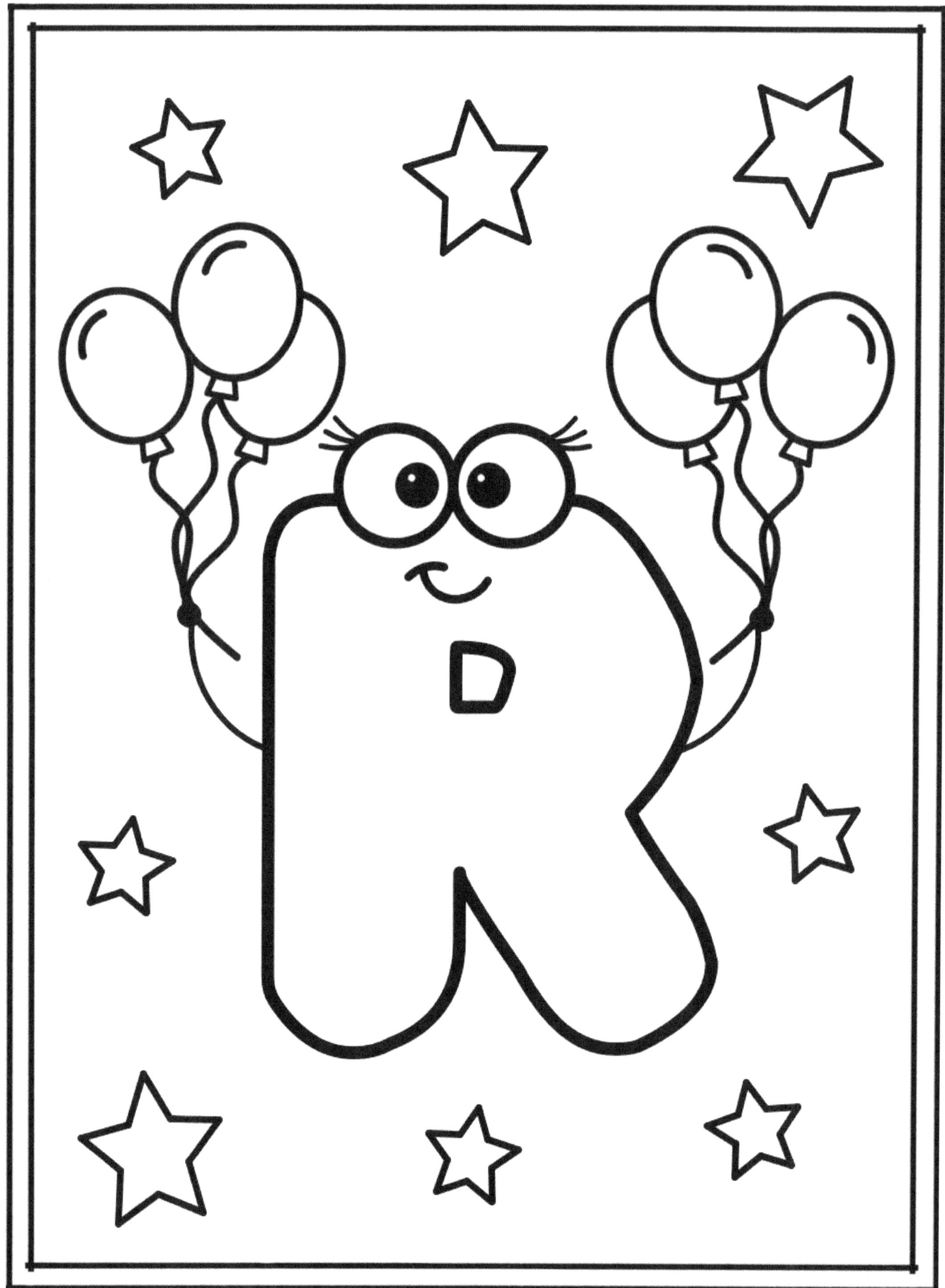

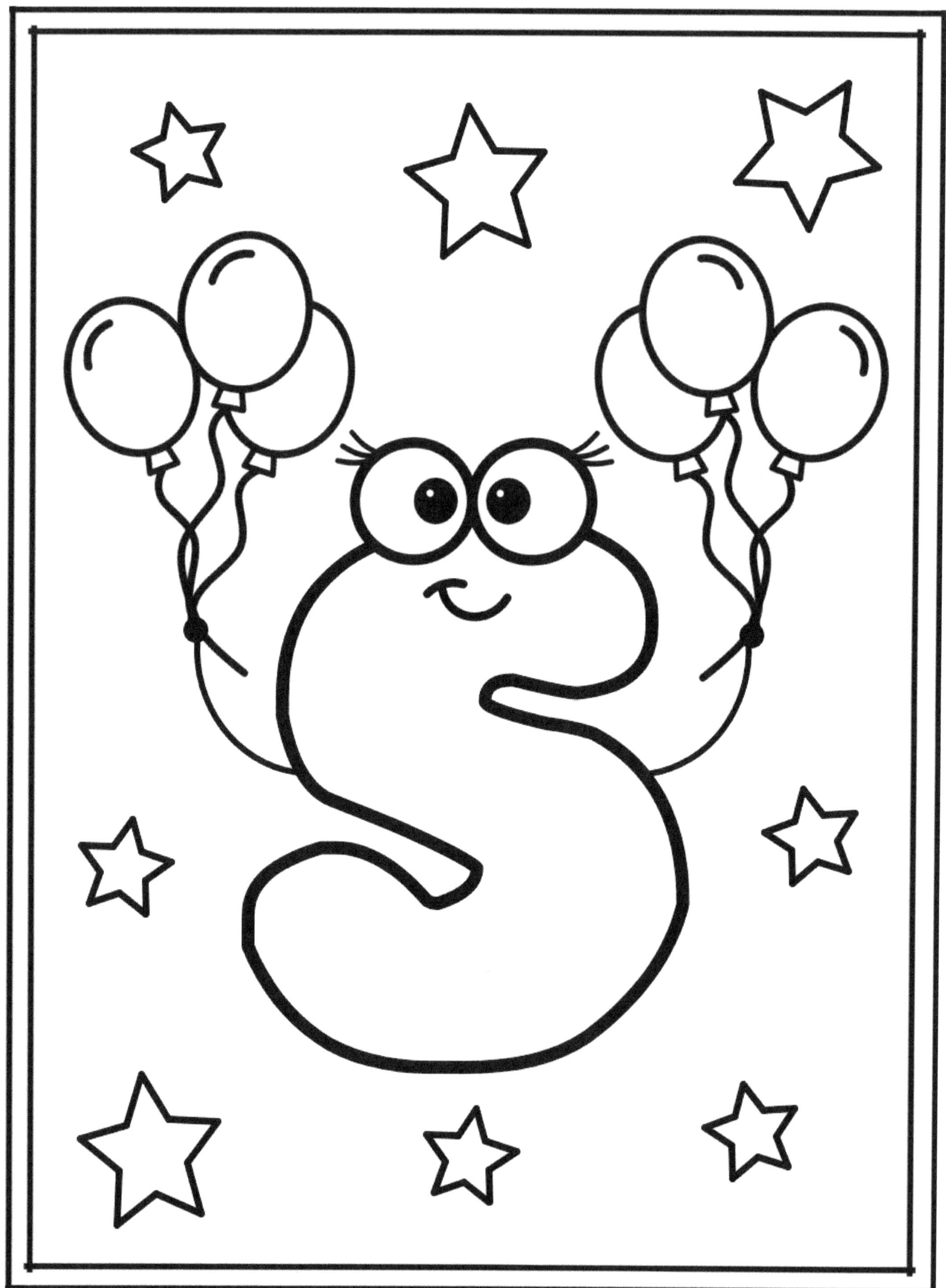

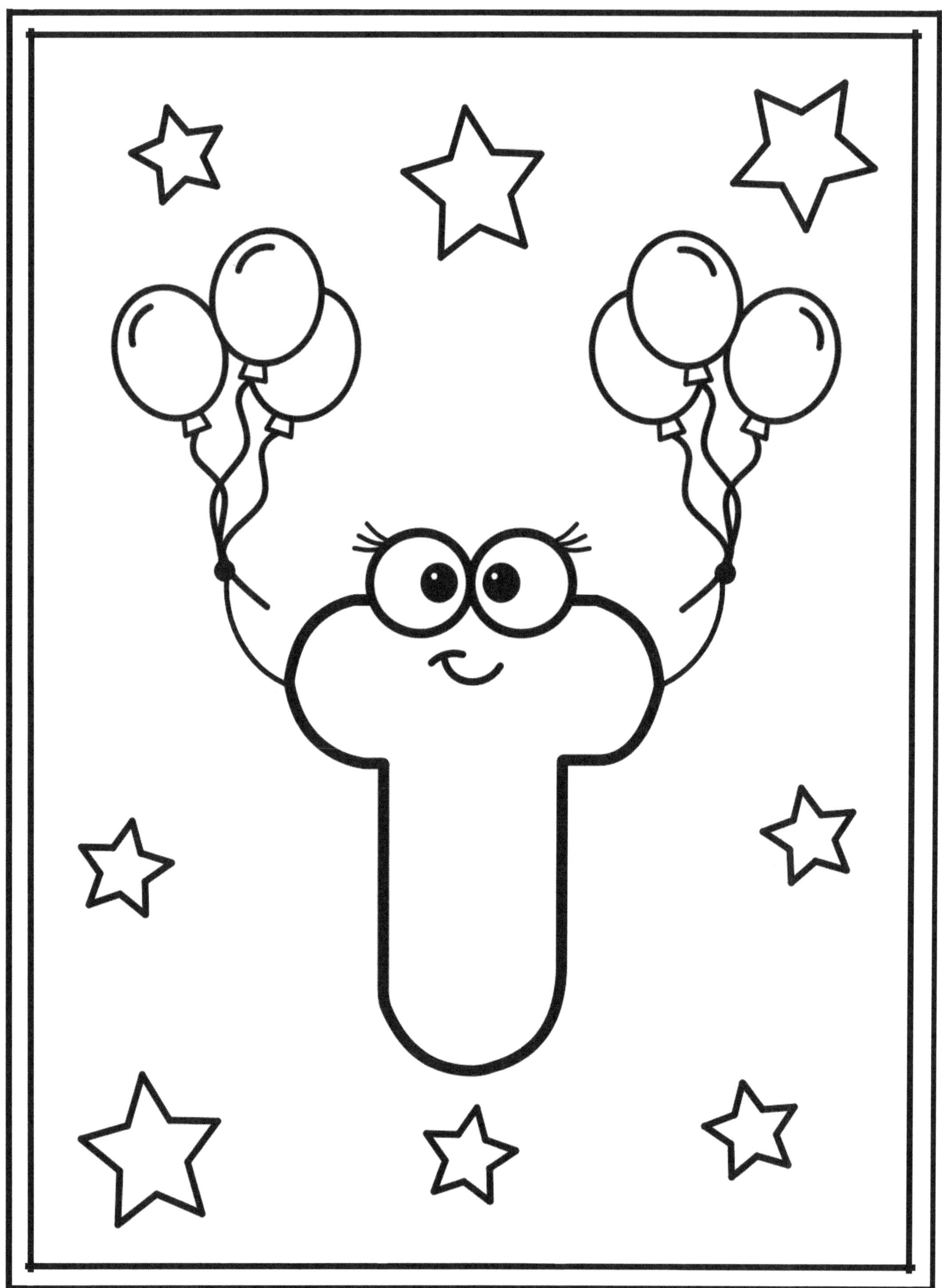

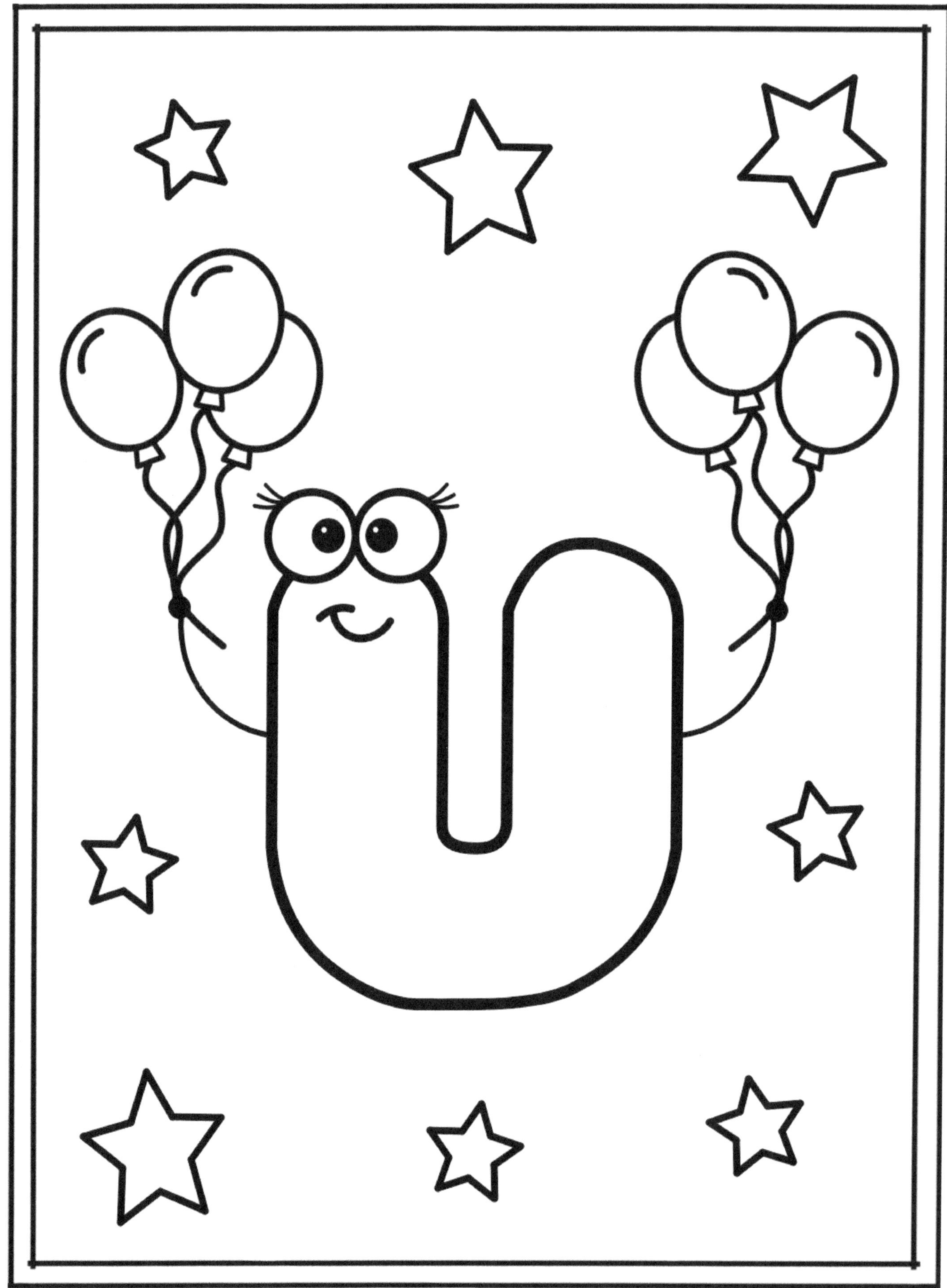

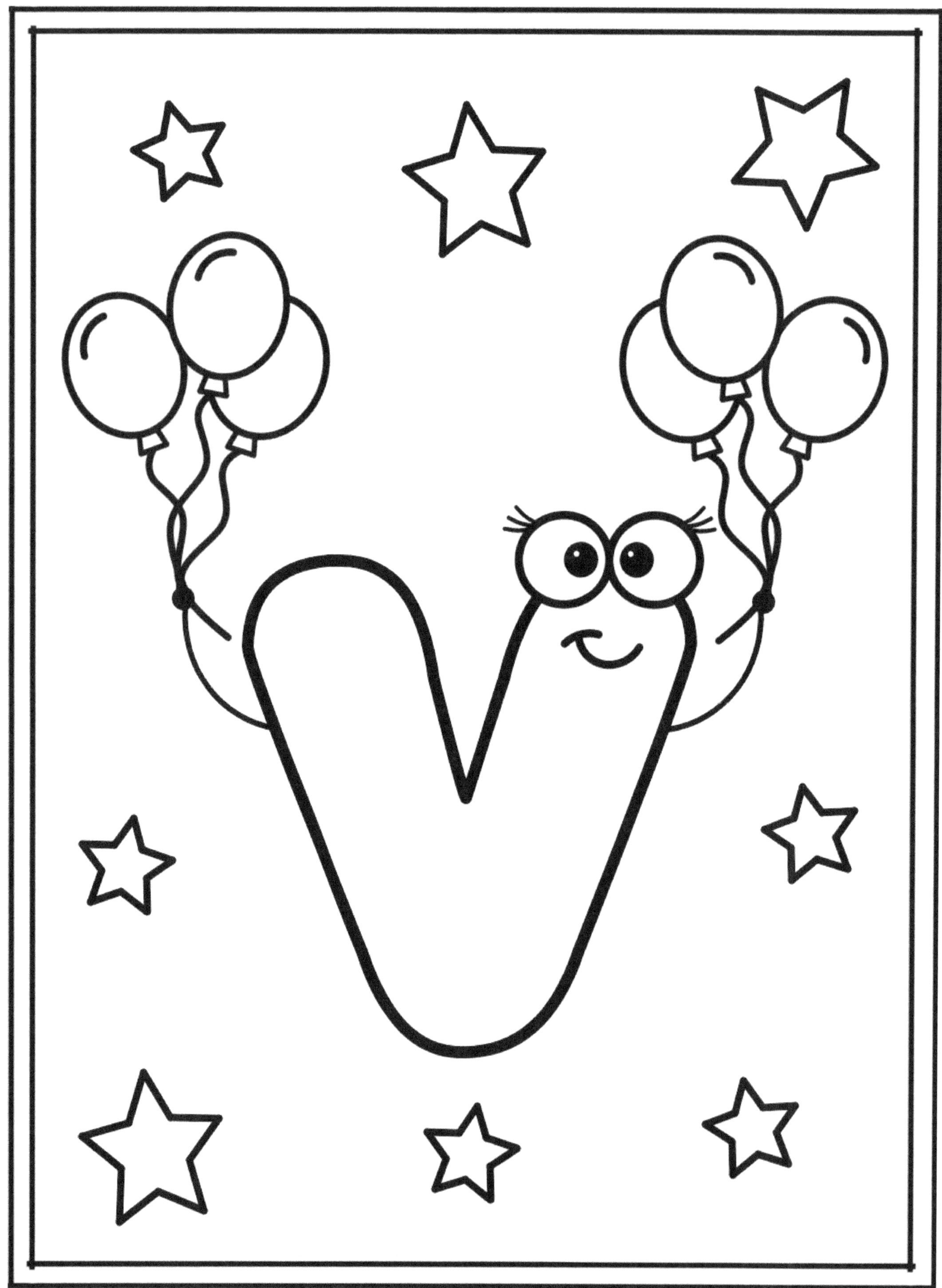

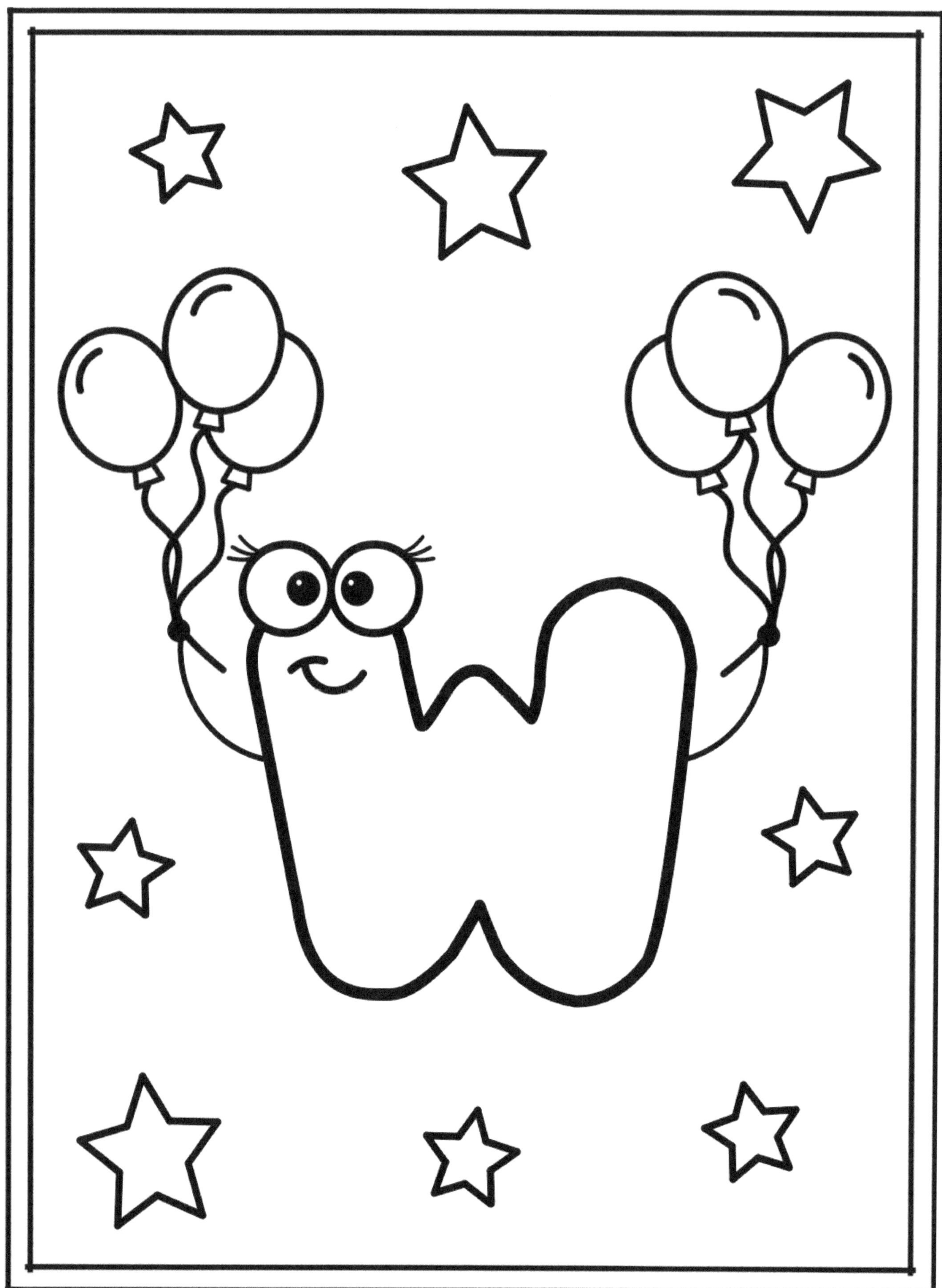

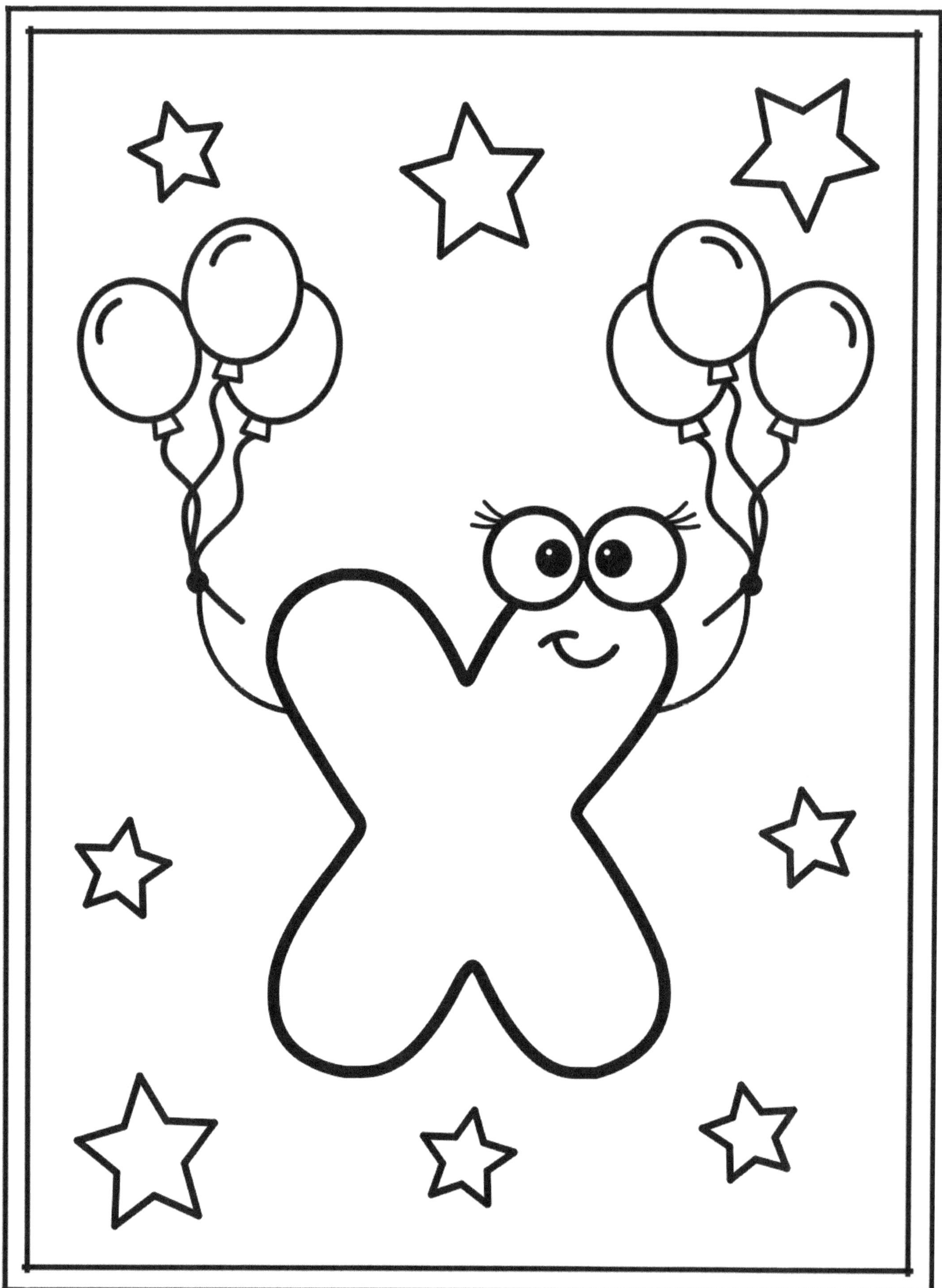

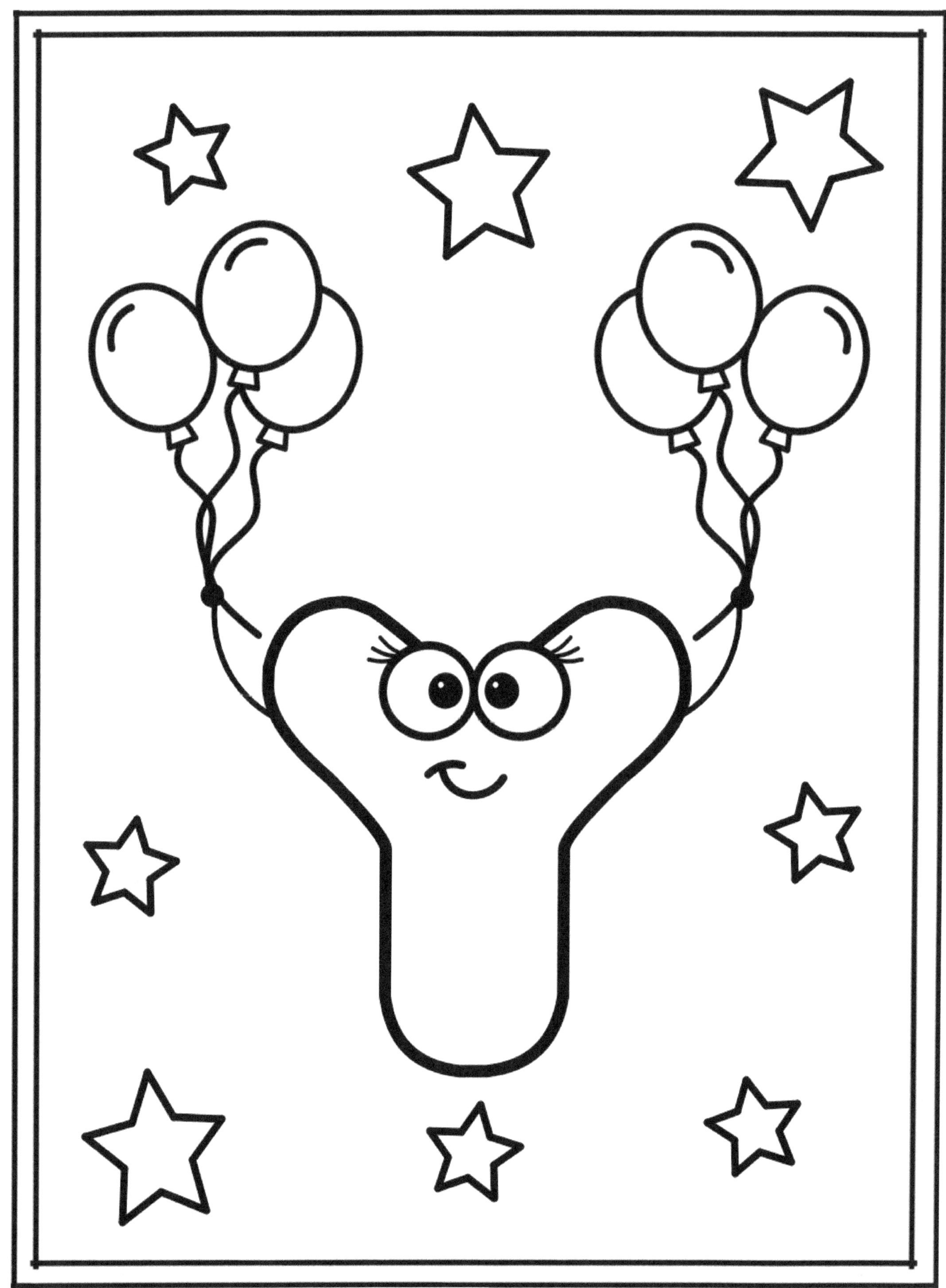

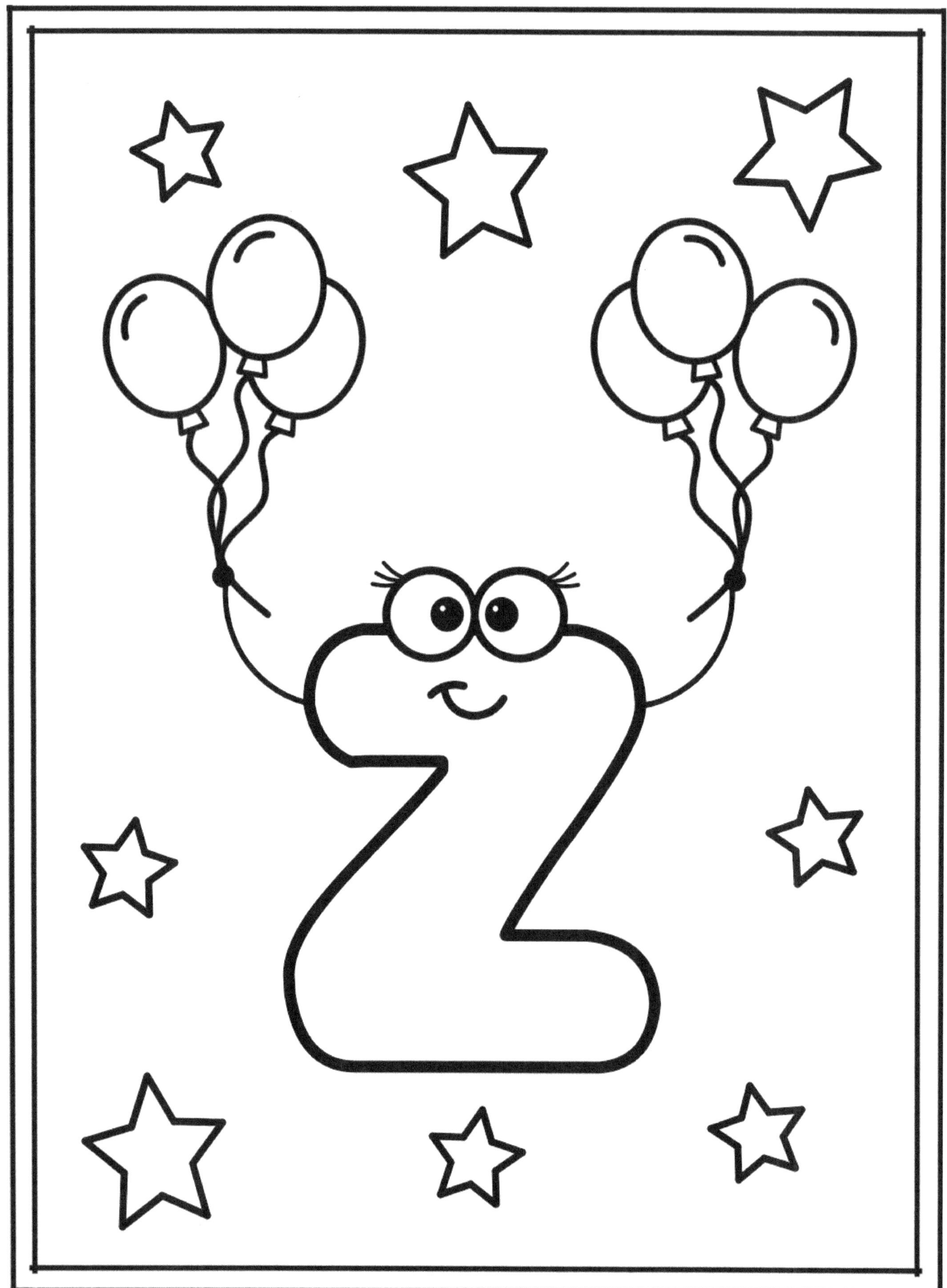

Excellent

work